4/2012

RESCUING Animals
FROM DISASTERS

SAVING ANIMALS AFTER TORNADOES

by Stephen Person

Consultants:

Sandra Allinson
Director of Education
Alabama Wildlife Center
Pelham, Alabama

Allison Graves
Have a Heart Animal Rescue and Adoption
Birmingham, Alabama

Janine Woods
Director, Mobile SPCA
Mobile, Alabama

BEARPORT
PUBLISHING

New York, New York

Credits

Cover and Title Page, © Jeff Haller/Keyhole Photo/Corbis; 4, © Willoughby Owen/Flickr/Getty Images; 5, © AP Photo/ Dave Martin; 6, © Marvin Gentry/Reuters/Landov; 7, © Vulcan Park Animal Care; 8, © AP Photo/Dave Martin; 10T, © Larry W. Smith/EPA/Landov; 10B, © Butterworth/Splash News/Newscom; 11, © AP Photo/The Tuscaloosa News/Dusty Compton; 12, © Christine Kneidinger Hull/al.com; 13, © Chuck Cook/The Humane Society of the United States; 14L, © AP Photo/Dave Martin; 14R, © AP Photo/Charlie Riedel; 15, © Phil Doster, Birmingham, AL; 16, © AP Photo/Dave Martin; 17T, © The North Shore Animal League America; 17B, © The North Shore Animal League America, photo by AJ Mast; 18, © Andrew Yeager; 19, © Andrew Yeager; 20L, © Rick Meyer/UPI/Newscom; 20R, © AP Photo/Charlie Riedel; 21, © AP Photo/Charlie Riedel; 22, © AP Photo/Mark Schiefelbein; 23, © 2011, The American Society for the Prevention of Cruelty to Animals (ASPCA). All Rights Reserved; 24, © Edd Cote/PATCH.Com; 25, © Edd Cote/PATCH.Com; 26, © The Everett Collection; 27, © Ted Fitzgerald/Boston Herald; 28, © Tim Woodward of Animal Rescue Corps; 29T, © Birdchick.com; 29B, © Nikki Tundel, Minnesota Public Radio.org; 31, © Willoughby Owen/Flickr/Getty Images.

Publisher: Kenn Goin
Editorial Director: Adam Siegel
Creative Director: Spencer Brinker
Design: Dawn Beard Creative and Kim Jones
Photo Researcher: Picture Perfect Professionals, LLC

Library of Congress Cataloging-in-Publication Data

Person, Stephen.
   Saving animals after tornadoes / by Stephen Person.
       p. cm. — (Rescuing animals from disasters)
   Includes bibliographical references and index.
   ISBN-13: 978-1-61772-458-9 (library binding)
   ISBN-10: 1-61772-458-0 (library binding)
   1. Animal rescue—Juvenile literature. 2. Tornadoes—Juvenile literature. 3. Animal welfare—United States—Societies, etc.—Juvenile literature. I. Title.
   HV4708.P467 2012
   636.08′32—dc23
                                        2011036124

For more information, write to Bearport Publishing Company, Inc., 45 West 21st Street, Suite 3B, New York, New York 10010. Printed in the United States of America in North Mankato, Minnesota.

10 9 8 7 6 5 4 3 2 1

CONTENTS

Mason Versus the Tornado

A young dog named Mason knew he was in serious danger. The date was April 27, 2011, and a powerful **tornado** was ripping through North Smithfield, a **suburb** of Birmingham, Alabama. Mason hid from the storm inside the garage of his family's home. Suddenly, the wind tore off the garage door. Mason was sucked outside and swept high into the air!

Tornadoes reach from thunderstorm clouds all the way down to the ground.

Tornadoes are among the most powerful storms in nature. They are violent swirling columns of air, with winds that can top 200 miles per hour (322 kph). Tornadoes usually move along the ground at about 30 miles per hour (48 kph) but can reach speeds up to 70 miles per hour (113 kph).

The tornado slammed Mason down to the ground far from his home. He tried to stand, but the bones in both of his front legs were broken. Unable to walk, Mason began crawling toward home, pushing his body forward with his **hind legs**. Without help, Mason would not survive.

Like Mason, this dog was separated from its owner when the tornado hit Alabama.

Rescued at Last

Mason's owners survived the storm, though their house was badly damaged. When the tornado passed, they went outside to look for Mason. He was nowhere in sight. After days of searching, the family gave up. They were sure they would never see their dog again. Then one day, about two and a half weeks later, the family got a big surprise. There, sitting on the porch, was Mason. He had gone so long without food he was down to just half his normal weight. Yet the little dog had still managed to crawl all the way home!

Tornadoes destroyed homes all over Birmingham, Alabama, on April 27, 2011.

The family rushed Mason to an animal hospital. A **veterinarian** named Bill Lamb and two other animal doctors worked on Mason for three and a half hours. They had to put two metal plates and 17 screws in Mason's legs to help them heal. The hard work paid off—Mason was soon able to begin walking again.

Mason standing on his bandaged legs after veterinarians fixed them

Mason became famous when his story appeared in newspapers and on television. People **donated** money to help Mason's family pay the dog's medical bills.

The Super Outbreak

Mason was lucky. He found his owners and was able to **recover**. Many other animals in the area were not so lucky. The tornado that destroyed Mason's neighborhood was just one of many to strike that day. In fact, **meteorologists** say that more than 300 tornadoes struck in 15 different states between April 26 and April 28, 2011.

This photo shows the destruction caused by one of the tornadoes in Tuscaloosa, Alabama.

When many tornadoes strike at once, it is called an **outbreak** of tornadoes. The outbreak at the end of April was so huge it became known as the Super Outbreak of 2011. More than 340 people were killed by the storms. The most severe damage was done in Alabama, where about 200 people died and thousands of buildings were flattened.

Super Outbreak of 2011

CANADA

UNITED STATES

WA
MT
ND
MN
OR
ID
WY
SD
WI
MI
ME
VT
NH
MA
NY
RI
CT
PA
NJ
NV
UT
CO
NE
IA
IL
IN
OH
WV
VA
DE
MD
CA
KS
MO
KY
NC
AZ
NM
OK
AR
TN
SC
Atlantic Ocean
Pacific Ocean
TX
LA
MS
AL
GA
FL
Gulf of Mexico
MEXICO

N
W E
S

☐ Where the tornadoes hit on April 27, 2011

Most of the world's tornadoes occur in the United States. An average of about 1,300 tornadoes hit the country each year.

During the Super Outbreak, tornadoes hit states from Mississippi all the way to New York.

Twisters and Animals

Tornadoes like the ones that slammed Alabama in 2011 are sometimes called **twisters**. That's because the spinning storms are twisting columns of air. Twisters can last anywhere from just a few seconds to an hour or more. Most, however, are over in less than ten minutes.

Scientists know that tornadoes are formed during powerful **thunderstorms**. It's still a mystery, however, why the violent winds of some thunderstorms create tornadoes while most do not.

Tornado winds are so strong they can knock down buildings, rip trees from the ground, and flip cars weighing 4,000 pounds (1,814 kg) or more.

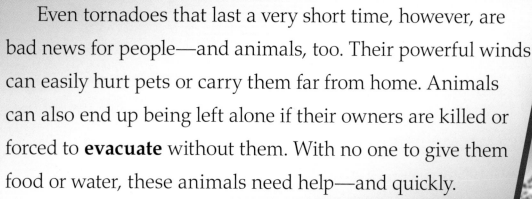

Even tornadoes that last a very short time, however, are bad news for people—and animals, too. Their powerful winds can easily hurt pets or carry them far from home. Animals can also end up being left alone if their owners are killed or forced to **evacuate** without them. With no one to give them food or water, these animals need help—and quickly.

A tornado destroyed this mother and daughter's home in Tuscaloosa, Alabama. Still, they felt lucky when they found their dog, Shadow, after the storm.

Rescuers on the Move

After the Super Outbreak of 2011, animal rescuers raced to the hardest-hit neighborhoods. Kimberly Gentry of the Alabama Society for the Prevention of Cruelty to Animals (ALSPCA) was one of the first to search the streets of Tuscaloosa. She saw heaps of wood and bricks where houses once stood—and near many of the piles were frightened, **injured** pets. "There are all kinds of dogs and cats wandering around," she told a reporter at the time.

This girl found her friend's kitten among the scattered remains of the family's home in Alabama.

Kimberly loaded the animals into vans and drove them to **animal shelters**. There, workers gave the pets food and water. Veterinarians worked day and night to treat the animals' injuries. Meanwhile, Kimberly went out to look for more animals in need of rescue. "We are not going to give up," she said, "because the animals need us more than ever."

This picture shows a worker from the Humane Society of the United States, another rescue group that helped animals after the 2011 tornadoes.

Established in 1954, the Humane Society of the United States is the country's largest animal protection organization.

Using the Internet

For weeks after the Super Outbreak of 2011, rescue workers continued to find animals and bring them to shelters. Saving the animals was just part of the job, however. The next step was to **reunite** pets with their owners. With so many pets separated from their families, how could this be done?

These puppies and kittens wait at shelters after the Super Outbreak of 2011 separated them from their owners.

The **Internet** was a huge help. The president of Have a Heart Animal Rescue and Adoption in Birmingham, Alabama, along with three other animal **advocates**, created a Facebook page called "Animals Lost & Found from the Tornadoes in Alabama on 4/27/11." Individuals and rescuers posted pictures of animals that they had lost or found. They included information about what shelters the animals had been taken to. Using this Facebook page, more than 100 families were able to find their lost pets.

Thanks to the efforts of Have a Heart Animal Rescue and Adoption, as well as the Facebook page, this dog was reunited with its owner.

Most of the pets that were posted on the Facebook page were dogs and cats. However, rescuers also posted pictures of lost birds, rabbits, guinea pigs, and other animals.

From Alabama to New York

Sadly, many pets could not be reunited with their owners. Some pet owners had died in the storm. Others had lost all their possessions and had no way to take care of their animals anymore. Shelters around Alabama were crowded with more than 1,000 animals in need of new homes. Something had to be done.

Workers from the Washington Animal Rescue League in Washington, D.C., took 37 homeless dogs from Alabama so that they could be adopted in the Washington, D.C., area.

This puppy waits for its owner in a shelter in Tuscaloosa, Alabama.

Animal rescuers from around the country responded. For example, a team from the North Shore Animal League America in Long Island, New York, jumped into their animal rescue bus. They drove all the way to Alabama and returned home with nearly 80 dogs and cats. The animals were given medical care and were soon **adopted** by families in New York.

These three puppies were among the animals rescued by the North Shore Animal League America.

The North Shore Animal League America rescuers call this bus their mobile rescue unit.

Birds in Danger

Pets were not the only animals in need of rescue after the Super Outbreak. When people walked through the parks, backyards, and woods near Birmingham, they realized wild birds were also in danger. The storm had blown down many trees, tossing baby birds and their parents out of the branches and down to the ground. Hundreds of birds had broken wings or damaged feathers.

A rescuer feeds this baby robin a healthy mix of cat food, yogurt, and vitamins.

Without quick help, the birds would have starved to death or been eaten by **predators** such as foxes, snakes, and raccoons. To save the wounded birds, **volunteers** from the Alabama **Wildlife** Center put them in cardboard boxes and took them to their facility. There, the birds were fed by hand and kept safe while they healed. When the birds were strong enough, they were released back into the wild.

A rescue worker from the Alabama Wildlife Center checks this rescued baby owl for injuries.

Tornadoes are very dangerous to baby birds. Most types of birds cannot fly until they are a few weeks old. As a result, baby birds are not able to move to safety if they see tornadoes coming.

19

Another Killer Storm

Less than a month after the Super Outbreak of 2011, a massive tornado hit the city of Joplin, Missouri, on May 22. The storm flattened entire neighborhoods, killing more than 100 people. Animal rescuers, like Debbie Hill of the Humane Society of Missouri, knew that hundreds of animals were out there in need of help. It's very important "to get in as quick as you can," she said.

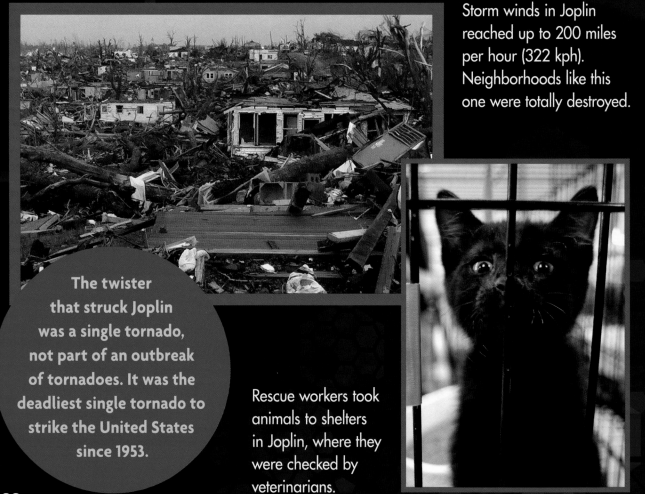

Storm winds in Joplin reached up to 200 miles per hour (322 kph). Neighborhoods like this one were totally destroyed.

The twister that struck Joplin was a single tornado, not part of an outbreak of tornadoes. It was the deadliest single tornado to strike the United States since 1953.

Rescue workers took animals to shelters in Joplin, where they were checked by veterinarians.

Debbie and other rescuers spent days driving through the **deserted** streets, searching for animal survivors. "We are often the last hope for animals that are left behind," said Debbie, "and that's why we won't leave until the job is done."

This woman holds a ferret she rescued after the tornado in Joplin destroyed the animal's house.

Dogs Saving Dogs

Rescuers, like Debbie Hill, knew that animals had survived the tornado, but they weren't always easy to find. That's why rescue teams in Joplin used **search-and-rescue dogs**. These dogs are specially trained to use their strong senses of smell and hearing to find survivors after disasters.

This rescue dog and worker searched for survivors in what was left of an apartment building in Joplin, Missouri.

Five days after the storm, a search-and-rescue dog named Javier jumped onto a pile of **rubble** that had once been a home. He sniffed around for a while, then suddenly stopped, turned to human rescuers, and barked. The people climbed onto the pile and listened. A faint moaning could be heard from under the wood and broken glass. The team tried to get closer to the sound by carefully pulling **debris** off the pile. Soon a dog squirmed out—frightened and very hungry, but not badly hurt.

After the Joplin tornado, the ASPCA and the Joplin Humane Society decided to hold an "adopt-a-thon"—a two-day event for the animals left homeless by the storm. More than 5,000 people from 24 states came to the event. Around 745 pets found new homes.

This puppy found a new family to go home with at the ASPCA's adopt-a-thon in Joplin. He also got a new name—Joplin.

Saving Cajun

Tornadoes continued to pound the country through the spring of 2011, with another big storm hitting western and central Massachusetts on June 1. Joann Kass and Steven Bush worried a twister would hit their barn and kill the horses inside. To save them, Joann and Steven threw the barn doors open, letting the four horses out. Then Joann and Steve dove into the **cellar** beneath their house, where they hoped they would be safe.

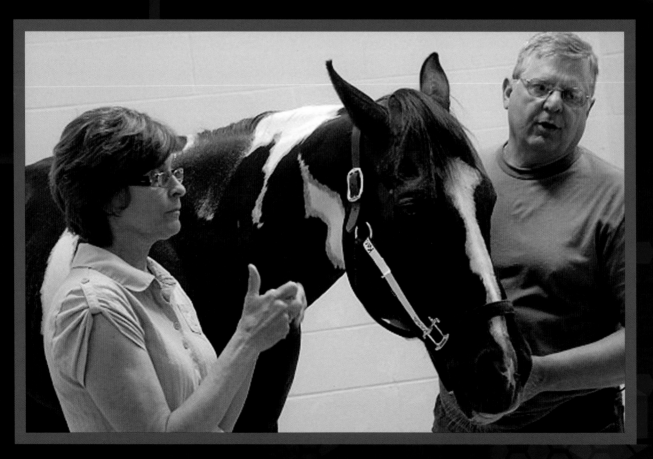

Joann Kass and Steven Bush with their horse Cajun

After the tornado passed, Joann and Steven came out of the cellar. They saw that their barn had been turned into a heap of cracked **lumber**. Had their horses been harmed as well? Joann and Steven quickly searched the nearby woods. They soon found one of their horses, Cajun, but he was bleeding badly. The wind had driven a sharp stick into his right back leg. Steven and Joann drove the wounded horse to an animal hospital. During a two-hour operation, veterinarians were able to clean his wound and repair his leg. Cajun was soon able to begin walking again.

One of the vets who treated Cajun holds a cup filled with wooden splinters that were taken out of the horse's leg.

Several vets volunteered to work on Cajun without pay.

Toto's New Family

A few days after the tornadoes hit Massachusetts, a worker who was cleaning up some fallen trees saw something incredible. Clinging to a branch was a tiny three-week-old kitten. A firefighter brought the kitten to the Animal Rescue League of Boston where workers there named the kitten Toto.

Toto was named after the dog in the famous novel *The Wonderful Wizard of Oz*, written in 1900 by L. Frank Baum. In this book, Toto is carried away by a tornado.

A scene from the 1939 movie *The Wizard of Oz* shows Toto and his owner, Dorothy.

Kittens that are as young as Toto are still **nursing**. Without their mother's milk they will starve to death. As a result, workers at the Animal Rescue League of Boston fed Toto milk from a baby bottle—but then they had a better idea. They placed Toto in a cage with a mother cat that had just given birth to kittens. In no time at all Toto was nursing alongside his new brothers and sisters. One of the tornado's smallest victims was safe at last with his new family.

Toto was cared for by rescue workers from the Animal Rescue League of Boston.

FAMOUS TORNADOES AND RESCUES

The Super Outbreak of 2011 was one of the deadliest tornado outbreaks in United States history. It was just one of many outbreaks, however, that have put animals in danger.

Oklahoma-Kansas Outbreak, May 3, 1999

- A total of 74 tornadoes hit Oklahoma and Kansas in one day, killing 46 people and damaging thousands of buildings.

- Many horses were injured in the storm. Veterinarian Michael J. Wiley treated the horses for little or no pay, while volunteers helped by feeding the horses and cleaning their stalls.

- Rescuers with the Oklahoma City Animal Shelter took in lost pets and gave them medical care.

Guthrie, Oklahoma, May 24, 2011

An Animal Rescue Corps worker saved this puppy after tornadoes struck Guthrie, Oklahoma.

- Several tornadoes hit the city of Guthrie, Oklahoma. One of the buildings hit by the storm was the Guthrie Animal Shelter.

- More than 60 cats and dogs were in the building when the storm hit. Amazingly, they all survived—even though the building was destroyed.

- Rescuers from Animal Rescue Corps rushed to Guthrie to help. They picked up the cats and dogs and drove them to animal shelters that had not been damaged by the tornadoes.

ANIMALS AT RISK FROM TORNADOES

Animal rescuers work quickly to save dogs, cats, and other family pets from tornadoes. However, these powerful storms can also put farm animals and wildlife in danger—and in need of rescue.

Farm Animals

- Farm animals, such as horses, cows, and chickens, can be injured when tornadoes cause barns or other farm buildings to fall down. Animals can also be hit by flying debris, such as tree branches.
- If farmers are killed or forced to evacuate their farms, animals living there may be left without food and water.
- After the Super Outbreak of 2011, rescuers drove from farm to farm, bringing food and fresh water to animals in need. Veterinarians traveled to farms to treat injured animals.

Wildlife

- Tornadoes can kill or injure wild animals. The storms can also destroy the **habitats** on which these animals depend.

This injured baby deer was found after a tornado hit Minneapolis.

- In May 2011, a tornado hit Minneapolis, Minnesota. The storm knocked down hundreds of trees in a park, destroying the great blue heron nests that were there. Many baby birds were in danger of starving.
- Rescuers gathered the young herons and took them to a wildlife center, where they were fed and checked by vets. Two months later, when the birds were strong enough to live on their own, they were released back into the wild.

This great blue heron was released into the wild in Minnesota.

GLOSSARY

adopted (uh-DOPT-id) taken into one's family

advocates (AD-vuh-kits) people who support or speak in favor of something

animal shelters (AN-uh-muhl SHEL-turz) places where homeless animals can stay until they find new homes

cellar (SEL-ur) a room below ground level in a house, often used to store things or as a safe place to stay during storms

debris (duh-BREE) scattered pieces of houses, buildings, and other objects that have been broken or destroyed

deserted (di-ZUR-tid) having no people living in an area

donated (DOH-nayt-id) gave something as a gift

evacuate (i-VAK-yoo-*ayt*) move away from an area that is dangerous

habitats (HAB-uh-*tats*) the places in nature where a plant or animal normally lives

hind legs (HYEND LEGS) back legs

injured (IN-jurd) hurt

Internet (IN-tur-net) a system of computer networks that connects billions of people all over the world

lumber (LUHM-bur) wood used for building things

meteorologists (mee-tee-ur-OL-uh-jists) scientists who study and forecast the weather

nursing (NURS-ing) drinking milk from one's mother

outbreak (OUT-*brayk*) a sudden increase in the activity of something

predators (PRED-uh-turz) animals that hunt and kill other animals for food

recover (ri-KOV-ur) to get better after an injury or illness

reunite (*ree*-yoo-NITE) to bring together again after being apart

rubble (RUHB-uhl) broken pieces of rock, brick, and other building materials

search-and-rescue dogs (SURCH-AND-RES-kyoo DAWGZ) dogs that look for survivors after a disaster, such as an earthquake or a tornado

suburb (SUHB-urb) an area of homes and businesses close to a city

thunderstorms (THUHN-dur-*stormz*) storms with thunder and lightning

tornado (tor-NAY-doh) a violent, whirling column of air that moves over the land and can cause much destruction

twisters (TWIST-urz) another word for *tornadoes*

veterinarian (*vet*-ur-uh-NAIR-ee-uhn) a doctor who cares for animals

volunteers (*vol*-uhn-TIHRZ) people who offer to do a job without pay

wildlife (WILDE-life) wild animals living in their natural environment

BIBLIOGRAPHY

Alabama Wildlife Center (www.awrc.org)

Animal Rescue Corps (www.animalrescuecorps.org/about-us/)

Have a Heart Animal Rescue and Adoption
(www.haveaheartanimalrescue.com/)

Joplin Humane Society (www.joplinhumane.org/)

The Online Tornado FAQ (www.spc.noaa.gov/faq/tornado/#The%20Basics)

READ MORE

Ball, Jacqueline A. *Tornado! The 1974 Super Outbreak (X-treme Disasters That Changed America).* New York: Bearport (2005).

Gibbons, Gail. *Tornadoes!* New York: Holiday House (2010).

Rudolph, Jessica. *Erased by a Tornado! (Disaster Survivors).* New York: Bearport (2010).

Woods, Michael and Mary B. *Tornadoes.* Minneapolis, MN: Lerner (2007).

LEARN MORE ONLINE

To learn more about saving animals after tornadoes, visit
www.bearportpublishing.com/RescuingAnimalsfromDisasters

INDEX

ABOUT THE AUTHOR

Stephen Person has written many children's books about history, science, and the environment. He lives with his family in Saratoga Springs, New York.